WITHDRAWN

A Yes-or-No Answer

A Yes-or-No Answer

JANE SHORE

Houghton Mifflin Company

Boston • *New York*

2008

For information about permission to reproduce selections from
this book, write to Permissions, Houghton Mifflin Company,
215 Park Avenue South, New York, New York 10003.

www.houghtonmifflinbooks.com

Library of Congress Cataloging-in-Publication Data
Shore, Jane, date.
A yes-or-no answer / Jane Shore.
p.   cm.
ISBN 978-0-547-00603-1
I. Title.
PS3569.H5795Y47 2008
811'.54 — dc22   2008001529

Printed in the United States of America

Book design by Robert Overholtzer

WOZ 10 9 8 7 6 5 4 3 2 1

Grateful acknowledgment is made to the editors of the following publications in
which these poems first appeared, sometimes in slightly different form.

The New Yorker: "Possession." *Ploughshares:* "My Mother's Foot," "Trick Candles."
Poet Lore: "My Daughter Reads My Old Diary," "Rattlesnake." *Pequod:* "Trouble
Dolls." *Salmagundi:* "The Streak," "My Father's Visits," "September, 9, 1995." *Tikkun:*
"Body and Soul." *TriQuarterly:* "Gelato," "The Mausoleum." *The Women's Review
of Books:* "My Mother's Chair," "Ode to Utensils."

"Scrabble in Heaven" was first published in *Princeton University Library Chronicles,*
vol. 63, nos. 1–2 (Autumn 2001–Winter 2002), edited by C. K. Williams. "The Closet"
previously appeared in *Poets of the New Century,* edited by Roger Weingarten and
Richard Higgerson (Boston: David R. Godine, 2001).

And thank you to Lorrie Goldensohn, Barry Goldensohn, Jody Bolz, Linda Pastan,
Joyce Johnson, Nadell Fishman, Stanley Plumly, Tony Hoagland, Julie Agoos, and
Ellen Voigt. And to my editor, Michael Collier.

EMMA

I'll forgive and I'll forget, but I'll remember.

—YIDDISH PROVERB

CONTENTS

I

A YES-OR-NO ANSWER

Have you read *The Story of O*?
Will Buffalo sink under all that snow?
Do you double-dip your Oreo?
Please answer the question yes or no.

The surgery — was it touch-and-go?
Does a corpse's hair continue to grow?
Remember when we were simpatico?
Answer my question: yes or no.

Do you want another cup of joe?
If I touch you, is it apropos?
Are you certain that you're hetero?
Is your answer yes or no?

Did you lie to me, like Pinocchio?
Was forbidden fruit the cause of woe?
Did you ever sleep with that so-and-so?
Just answer the question: yes or no.

Did you nail her under the mistletoe?
Will you spare me the details, blow by blow?
Did she sing sweeter than a vireo?
I need an answer. Yes or no?

Are we still a dog-and-pony show?
Shall we change partners and do-si-do?
Are you planning on the old heave-ho?
Check an answer: Yes ❏ No ❏.

Was something blue in my trousseau?
Do you take this man, this woman? Oh,
but that was very long ago.
Did we say yes? Did we say no?

For better or for worse? Ergo,
shall we play it over, in slow mo?
Do you love me? Do you know?
Maybe yes. Maybe no.

THE STREAK

Because she wanted it so much, because
she'd campaigned all spring and half the summer,
because she was twelve and was old enough,
because she would be responsible and pay for it herself,
because it was her mantra, breakfast, lunch, and dinner,
because she would do it even if we said no —

her father and I argued until we finally said
okay, just a little one in the front
and don't ask for any more, and, also,
no double pierces in the future, is that a deal?

She couldn't wait, we drove straight to town,
not to our regular beauty parlor, but the freaky one —
half halfway house, half community center —
where they showed her the sample card of swatches,
each silky hank a flame-tipped paintbrush dipped in dye.

I said no to Deadly Nightshade. No to Purple Haze.
No to Atomic Turquoise. To Green Envy. To Electric Lava
that glows neon orange under black light.
No to Fuchsia Shock. To Black-and-Blue.
To Pomegranate Punk. I vetoed Virgin Snow.
And so she pulled a five out of her wallet, plus the tax,
and chose the bottle of dye she carried carefully
all the car ride home, like a little glass vial
of blood drawn warm from her arm.

Oh she was hurrying me! Darting up the stairs,
double-locking the bathroom door,
opening it an hour later, sidling up to me, saying, "Well?"
For a second, I thought that she'd somehow
gashed her scalp. But it was only her streak, Vampire Red.

Later, brushing my teeth, I saw her mess —
the splotches where dye splashed
and stained the porcelain, and in the waste bin,
Kleenex wadded up like bloodied sanitary napkins.
I saw my girl — Persephone carried off to Hell,
who left behind a mash of petals on the trampled soil.

RATTLESNAKE

Only one day left of Christmas week,
one more long day I'd have to stay
with my great-aunt Sadie
while my parents were busy working.
We played gin rummy all afternoon,
gambling for pennies in her smoky kitchen.

She gave me a pack of "Licky Strikes" —
the red bull's-eye on the wrapper
exactly like the brand she smoked.
I peeled the red artery of cellophane,
tore the foil lining. Inside,
my candy cigarettes looked like
twenty sticks of pink-tipped chalk.
"Don't smoke them all at once," she joked.

At six o'clock, we ate dinner
on rickety tray tables
in front of the black-and-white TV.
Sadie ladled something onto my plate:
long as a sausage, delicate, bony
along the spine, fishy white flesh
threaded with gray spider-veins
like the veins webbing Aunt Sadie's pale thighs.
"Rattlesnake," she winked, smacking her lips.

I stared at my white plate
and the white piece of rattlesnake.
I poked at it, to be polite,
but my mouth was basted shut.
Aunt Sadie sat marble-still.

Sneaking peeks at her whiskery chin,
I waited for her to snip

the rubber band wound around
my ponytail — long, luxuriant,
my sole accomplishment —
and brush my hair one hundred strokes
as she had brushed my mother's hair
when my mother was a little girl.
But tonight, I slunk off to bed hungry,
my ponytail in snarls.

Next morning, shuffling the cards,
Aunt Sadie frowned.
"What do you need all that hair for?"
She jumped up, yanked open a drawer,
and with a pair of kitchen shears
she lopped off my ponytail
in one big hank, the rubber band
still holding it together.

It lay coiled on the floor.
Mine. Not mine.
She made me pick it up
and throw it in the trash.

But bending down, I felt it
flick the back of my neck
like the tail of a stubborn horse.

My mother was going to be furious.

MY MOTHER'S CHAIR

Coming home late, I'd let myself in
with my key, tiptoe up the stairs,
and there she was, in the family room,
one lamp burning, reading her newspaper
in her velvet-and-chrome swivel chair

as though it were perfectly natural
to be wide awake at 2 A.M.,
feet propped on the matching
ottoman, her orthopedic shoes
underneath, two empty turtle shells.

Like a mummy equipped for the afterlife,
she'd have her ashtray and Kents handy,
her magnifying mirror,
and tweezers and eyeglass case,
her crossword puzzle dictionary.

Glancing up and down, she never
appeared to be frisking me, even when,
just seconds before, coming home
from a date, at the front door,
I'd stuck my tongue into a boy's mouth.

I'd sit on the sofa and bum her cigarettes,
and as the room filled up with smoke,
melding our opposite temperaments,
we'd talk into the night, like diplomats
agreeing to a kind of peace.

I'd feign indifference — so did she —
about what I was doing out so late.
When I became a mother myself,
my mother was still the sentry at the gate,
waiting up, guarding the bedrooms.

After her funeral, her chair sat empty.
My father, sister, husband, and I
couldn't bring ourselves to occupy it.
Only my daughter climbed up its base
and spun herself round and round.

In the two years my father lived alone
in the apartment over their store,
I wonder, did he ever once
sit down on that throne, hub
around which our family had revolved.

After my father died, the night
before I left the place for good,
the building sold, the papers signed,
before the moving vans drove away,
dividing the cartons and the furniture

between my sister's house and mine,
a thousand miles apart,
I sat on the sofa — my usual spot —
and stared at the blank TV, the empty chair;
then I rose, and walked across the room,

and sank into her ragged cushions,
put my feet up on her ottoman,
rested my elbows on the scuffed armrests,
stroked the brown velvet like fur.
The headrest still smelled like her!

Swiveling the chair to face the sofa,
I looked at things from her point of view:
What do you need it for?
So I left it behind, along with the blinds,
the meat grinder, the pressure cooker.

THE CLOSET

Wearing her baby-blue nylon nightgown,
not the muslin shroud we buried her in,
my mother stands before my closet, puzzled.
Why are *her* dresses mingling with mine?

For once, my mother doesn't talk.
She bears no message from Jewish heaven
where the dead have nothing to do all day
but sit around and advise the living.
More like the Ten Commandments:
Never wear white in winter or velvet in summer.
Buy life insurance. File a will.

Does she want me to choose an outfit for her?
This is a first. *She* was always the expert on clothes.
Perhaps when you die, the first thing to go
is your fashion sense, because in Paradise
everyone's dressed the same.

I remember how, in her store, she'd
run her eyes over the racks of merchandise
and know exactly which dress
her customers should wear
to their fundraisers, cocktail parties, christenings.

But where's she going that's so important?
Since she's lost all that weight
her dresses would just hang off her,
so she might as well be naked.
Yet her eyes seem to be begging me
to help her, help her slip back again
into the shackles of clothes.

ODE TO UTENSILS

after Charlie Smith

Opening the drawer, I like the old-fashioned egg beater best,
green painted handle so worn and flaked
the blanched wood underneath shows through.
I like to see the evidence of another hand
beneath my own. I like how the twin rotors spin
in tandem, whipping up ghost breaths across my face.
I like the old apple corer and potato masher,
the ones you find at flea markets,
and the hinged egg slicer that, when opened,
is like the miniature lyre I used to pluck
playing in the corner of my mother's kitchen,
its perfect slices of cooked egg like cross sections
of boiled sun. I like the church key's one tooth
biting tin lids so that cans sigh with pleasure.
Strainers, funnels, slotted spoons, spatulas, ladles, tea balls
excite me. At night in bed, I swoon over catalogues of cookery,
and imagine my life as it will never be.
Utensils that sift flour, rice potatoes, plane cheese,
knives that are specialists, with blades
that pare and bone, fillet and carve —
gizmos that zest lemons, curl butter, strip an ear of corn
of its kernels, unravel its strands of silk —
cherry pitter, pepper mill, mortar and pestle, hand-cranked
grinder gnashing down chunks of raw meat and shitting
them out in one long continuous sentence —
peeler undressing the modest carrot, meat thermometer
stuck in the turkey's breast, barely grazing the wishbone —
O utensils, I like your tangs and tines and tongs and prongs.
Unlike me, you work without complaint.

When I close your drawer, do you pray in the dark
to your ancestors, those ancient scoops
made of horn and shell, socket and knuckle,
while I recline, cleaning my teeth with thorns?

POSSESSION

Nesting in my nest, she slept on my side
of the double bed, stacked the books — *my* books —
she was reading on my nightstand.
In the closet, her dresses pressed
against my husband's pants.
These I boxed up for her mother,
with the baby's toys.
I tossed her blue toothbrush
and her tortoiseshell comb in the trash.
Police took away a rug. My two best knives.

But the kitchen still smells of her spices —
her cinnamon, curry, cloves.
The house an aromatic maze
of incense and sachet.
Almost every day now something of hers
turns up. The way La Brea tar pits
keep disgorging ancient bones, squeezing them
through the oily black muscles of earth
to the surface.

A yoga mat.
I don't need it. I already have my own.
Prayer beads. A strapless bra.
A gold ring. It's pretty.
It fits my pinkie.

I wash my face with her special soap,
a cool oval of white clay,
one thick black hair still glued to it.
And is it wrong to brew her herbal teas, try her
aromatherapies, her homeopathic cures,

the Rescue Remedy she'd told me
really worked? The amber bottle's full.
Why waste it? So I deposit
four bitter drops on my own tongue.

TROUBLE DOLLS

*Guatemalan Indians tell of this old custom. When you have
troubles, remove one doll from the box for each problem. Before
you go to sleep, tell the doll your trouble. While you are sleeping,
the doll will try to solve it. Since there are only six dolls in a
box, you are allowed only six troubles a day.*

Every morning, I unbend
their wire limbs and lay them
back in their tiny box where
they sleep all day like vampires.

Their lidless eyes cannot close —
the pupils dots of black paint,
bull's-eyes ringed
with insomnia's dark circles.

Scalps sprinkled with black salt.
Arms opened wide,
as if expecting to be hugged
or crucified.

What were their troubles
before they came to me —
these brothers, husbands, wives,
this neighbor's son-in-law,

born in the old country
where churches collapsed
on their babies, and police
dragged off the baker,

soldiers raped the sister,
and a brother came home
with his arms twisted, and
the father with no arms at all?

Single file, they descend
the mineshaft of my unconscious,
with only a pickax and hardhat
beam to light their path.

Yet I worry that one night,
opening their box, I'll find
five dolls left, and the next night
four, subtracting a doll a day —

until, like the Disappeared,
they'll all vanish without a trace,
leaving me to worry all alone
in bed with their empty coffin.

THE BLUE ADDRESS BOOK

Like the other useless
things I can't bear
to get rid of — her
nylon nightgowns,

his gold-plated
cufflinks, his wooden
shoetrees, in a size
no one I know can use —

I'm stuck with their blue
pleather address book,
its twenty-six chapters
printed in ballpoint pen,

X'd out, penciled in,
and after she passed away,
amended in his hand,
recording, as in a family

Bible, those generations
born, married, and since
relocated to their graves:
Abramowitz to *Zimmerman.*

Great-uncles, aunts,
cousins once removed,
whose cheeks I kissed,
whose food I ate,

are in this book still
alive, immortal, each
name accompanied
by a face:

Fogel (Rose and Murray),
474 13th St., Brooklyn,
moved to a condo
in Boca Raton; *Stein*

(Minnie, sister of Rose),
left her Jerome Ave.
walk-up for the Yonkers
Jewish Nursing Home.

The baby-blue cover
has a patina of grease,
the pages steeped
in the cigarette smoke

of years spent in my
parents' junk drawer.
Though scattered
in different graveyards,

here they're all
accounted for.
Their souls disperse,
dust motes in the air

that I inhale.

II

A 440

The A above middle C is used to tune the instruments of the orchestra because, by international agreement, its pitch is set at a frequency of 440 cycles per second.

A squatter in my parents' house,
their Baldwin Acrosonic spinet
didn't leave home until my father died,
and having nowhere else to go,
was shipped here to my living room.

After ten years' sitting, it's out of tune,
the A mute, the damper pedal broken,
the B above middle C sunken in,
the battered walnut veneer embossed
like a notary's raised stamp.

The piano tuner unpacks the tools
stored in his rolling suitcase.
Sweeping generations of photos
from the dusty lid — Russian relatives,
my daughter's school portraits —

he stacks sheet music on the coffee table,
pulls out a silvery tuning fork
from his left breast pocket, bangs it
against his balding skull, holds it
to his good right ear, and listens hard,

refreshing his ear to the sound of A
above middle C, the piano's *axis mundi*.
I should leave, but mesmerized,
I watch his hairy arm and left hand
disappear inside the piano's innards,

cranking the tuning hammer this way
and that, moving the rubber mutes
along the strings, a little sharp,
a little flat, up and down the scale
while his right hand strikes the keys.

Two hours later, when he's gone,
on the piano bench lies a bill
twice higher than his estimate;
the lid wiped clean, the photos
approximate to where they were,

and also, fished out of the piano,
there's a three of clubs from a deck
I threw out years ago,
five pennies turned pewter gray,
a condolence card, the envelope

sealed with crackled yellow glue.
Its sender, now, has passed on, too.
It's been decades since I practiced
Für Elise or banged out torch songs
from *1,000 Standard Tunes,*

fakebook my father finagled from
his old musician buddies,
the boys he used to play with
in the big bands.
When I lost my father, I lost music.

When my daughter took lessons,
I'd sit beside her on the bench
just as my father once sat with me,
encouraging, correcting, wincing,
but I wouldn't play a single note.

The church bells across the street
begin to toll the quarter hour —
dividing my day, every day,
into bite-size intervals,
from seven in the morning

until seven at night, another
axis mundi. I find the key
and, instrument in tune, peck out
the melody to the first
Duet for Church Bells and Piano, opus 1.

THE MAUSOLEUM

On the yearly drive to the doctor,
my mother sometimes took me along for the ride,
the same route downhill on Bergen Boulevard
along the railroad tracks to Hackensack;
the Palisades, the Manhattan skyline at our backs —

you had to roll up your car windows
and hold your nose for hours, it seemed,
passing rusted trestles, oil drums
leaking poison rainbows in water still as stone,
which cattails, like tall straws, sucked —

I'd imagine a bird's-eye-view watercolor map
on which the buildings have been brushed away —
the amusement park, factories, the ugly
leaning Towers of Pizza, Mr. Donuts, Chicken Delights,
bar and grills, and used car lots;
weeds punching up through sidewalk cracks, crushing
the ragged jumble into a flat pastel —

I imagined them gone — the minuscule
two-family houses inching up the hillside's spine,
stoops, postage-stamp lawns with foot-tall
wrought-iron fences, jutting steeples brown-shingled, slate —
Our Lady of Libra, St. Joseph's —
dug up with a spade, and their surrounding streets with them,
repotted in the countryside, miles from there . . .

When we made the right-hand turn
and drove past the massive cinderblock of the mausoleum,
I'd glance at her — who, in the absence of talk
was humming a little something to herself,
she was still young, healthy, but one day . . .

I'd tuck that bad thought away, banishing it
to that part of the mind that holds its breath
as you drive past a graveyard, counting your heartbeats
until it's safe to breathe again.

MY DAUGHTER READS MY OLD DIARY

Like a needle stuck in the scratch of an old 45,
she keeps skipping back
to the boys I kissed and slow-danced with.
Reading the diary I kept when I was twelve,
my twelve-year-old feels entitled to the girl
I used to be, my past's her private property.
Puzzled, pursing her lips, sucking air
through the barbed filigree of her braces,
her purple polished fingernail grazes
a word scrawled in greasy blue ballpoint.
"Necking," I say, and she grins.
A serpent ring snakes down her index finger
stopping at "Spin the bottle." At twelve,
I kissed the boys, then kissed my dolls goodbye.
At twelve, she traded her bath toys
for a razor. Her legs are silken ivory.
She reads how I lied to my mother about
shaving mine, claiming those bloody nicks
on my shins were mosquito bites.
"God, Mom, you were *such* a baby!"
Shaking her head, she turns the page.

DUMMY

He lolled on my twin bed waiting for me
to get home from Girl Scouts or ballet,
but I couldn't really play with him
the way I'd played with my other dolls —
buttoning their dresses, buckling their shoes,
brushing and braiding their long, rooted curls.
He had the one crummy green gabardine suit.
His ketchup-colored hair was painted on.
And while my baby dolls could drink
from a bottle, cry real tears, blow bubbles,
and pee when I squeezed their tummies,
my dummy didn't have the plumbing.

The water bottles I'd jam in his mouth
scuffed his lipstick, mildewed his stuffing.
Prying his smile apart, I'd run my finger
along the seven milk teeth lining his jaw.
But look inside his head. Completely empty!
No tongue, no tonsils, no brain.
No wonder he had to wear his own name
on a label sewn above his jacket pocket
to remind himself that he was Jerry Mahoney
and his straight man an eleven-year-old girl
who jerked the dirty pull string at the back
of his neck, making his jaw drop open,

his chin clack like the Nutcracker's.
That lazy good-for-nothing! I had to put
words in his mouth. His legs hung limp,
his arms flopped at his sides. He couldn't
wink or blink or quit staring to the left;
brown eyes painted open, perpetually
surprised at what he'd blurt out next:
"Grandma Fanny has a big fat fanny!
Uncle Fred should lose that lousy toupee!

Aunt Shirley dresses like a goddamn tramp!
That son of hers, Moe, a moron!" —
what *they* said behind each other's backs!

He did a slow one-eighty of my bedroom.
"How the hell did I wind up in this joint?" —
that low, unnatural voice straining through
my own locked teeth. "Good evening, ladies,"
he leered at the dolls propped stiffly on the shelf,
cocking his head to see their underpants.
How old was that wiseacre supposed to be? —
thirteen? thirty? my father's age? — the little
man sitting on my lap, telling dirty jokes
until his pull string snapped, a fraying ganglion
lost inside his neck beyond the tweezers' reach,
a string of words unraveling down his throat.

After that, we practiced our act in the dark
where I couldn't see his imperfections.
We'd talk, long after the others were asleep:
I'd move my lips, lower my voice an octave;
and it almost sounded like a conversation
between a husband and a wife.
I tweaked his bow tie, smoothed his satin dickie,
rapped on his skull. *Knock, knock.* "Who's there?"
just like in the old days when he was in mint
condition, a smart aleck; before he became
slack-jawed, dumb — a dummy forever — and I
grew up, went solo, learned to speak for myself.

SHOPPING URBAN

Flip-flopped, noosed in puka beads, my daughter
breezes through the store from headband to toe ring,
shooing me away from the bongs,
lace thongs, and studded dog collars.
And I don't want to see her in that black muscle tee
with SLUT stamped in gold glitter
shrink-wrapped over her breasts,
or those brown and chartreuse retro-plaid
hip-huggers ripped at the crotch.

There's not a shopper here a day over twenty
except me and another mother
parked in chairs at the dressing room entrance
beyond which we are forbidden to go.
We're human clothes racks.
Our daughters have trained us
to tamp down the least flicker of enthusiasm
for the nice dress with room to grow into,
an item they regard with sullen, nauseated,
eyeball-rolling disdain.

Waiting in the line for a dressing room,
my daughter checks her cleavage.
Her bellybutton's a Cyclops eye
peeking at other girls' armloads of clothes.
What if she's missed something —
that faux leopard hoodie? those coffee-wash flares?
Sinking under her stash of blouses,
she's a Shiva of tangled sleeves.

And where did she dig up that new tie-dyed
tank top I threw away in '69,
and the purple wash 'n' wear psychedelic dress
I washed and wore

and lost on my Grand Tour of Europe,
and my retired hippie Peace necklace
now recycled, revived, re-hip?

I thought they were gone —
like the tutus and tiaras and wands
when she morphed from ballerina
to fairy princess to mermaid to tomboy,
refusing to wear dresses ever again.
Gone, those pastel party dresses,
the sleeves, puffed water wings buoying her up
as she swam into waters over her head.

MY MOTHER'S FOOT

Putting on my socks, I noticed,
on my right foot, an ugly bunion and hammertoes.
How did my mother's foot
become part of me? I thought I'd buried it
years ago with the rest of her body,
next to my father in Cedar Park Cemetery.
How did it ever track me down,
knowing exactly which brick house
on the street was mine,
never having set foot in it alive?

During dinner, my husband was polite.
My daughter excused herself to do homework.
When it got too late to phone a hotel,
I invited the foot to spend the night.
I made up the studio couch, tucked the foot in,
tiptoed back to my bedroom.
A minute later came a knock at my door.
I'm lonesome, the foot sobbed.
I'm not used to sleeping alone. Whereupon
it hopped into bed between my husband and me.

Next morning, the foot woke up
on the wrong side of the bed.
Its instep hurt. Its big toe was out of joint.
So I kissed it, gave it a pedicure,
polished its five wiggling toenails Madeira Red.
Life's really good here, the foot said.
So much better than where I've just come from.
Mind if I use your phone?
I've got a pal who has one foot in the grave.

That night, my mother's left foot joined us.
Now they're both giving me advice:

Your bathroom needs washing.
That dress makes you look fat.

Along with her pearls, her diamond ring,
and her gold earrings, I've got
my mother's knees, her varicose veins,
flabby belly, sagging breasts —

In time I'll inherit whatever's left of her body.

KEYS

What do I do with the Post-it notes
she stuck on the fridge?
Do I delete her e-mail asking
was it okay
if her little boy played
with my daughter's old keychains
stored in the shoebox under her bed?

Yes, of course. Be my guest.
While you're housesitting,
Mi casa es su casa, I said.
Then I showed her
how to lock the front door
and handed her the keys.

Such a nice little boy, said our neighbor.
Such an attentive mother.
Tony, the locksmith down the street,
would reach inside a grimy jar,
as if fishing for a candy,
and hand the boy another key or two —

a bent key, a worn-down key,
a key with broken teeth,
old mailbox keys, luggage keys, and sometimes
as a special treat he'd let the boy
choose a shiny blank from the rotating display
and cut him a brand-new key
to add to his collection.

The morning she locked the doors
and turned on the alarm,
and stabbed her son and slit her wrists
and lay down on my dining room floor

to die, she left a message
on my best friend's voice mail:
Let yourself in.
Bring your spare key . . .

Now, it's as if my house
keeps playing tricks on me.
I open my lingerie drawer and find a key.
Whose is it?
Which lock does it belong to?
I find a key under the coffee table.
A key wedged between sofa cushions.
A key with a tag to a '71 Chevy.
Cleaning under my daughter's bed,
I find rings of keys, lots more keys,
none of which fits any lock in my house.

TRICK CANDLES

after Cavafy

Flickering above the pink rosettes
and your name iced in ivory buttercream,
a bouquet burns on top of your cake,
fifty blossoms of flame.

One candle equals a year of your life,
plus one more to wish on.
Hurry, make a wish, blow them out!
They're out. Now cut the cake.

But wait — a guttered wick sputters and sparks
as if it suddenly has a mind of its own —
now another is lighting up,
and one by one, the dead reawaken.

Rekindled years return like little waves of nausea.
Here's 1947, the year you were born.
And 1956, when your mother had your sister.
Now 1993 joins the crowd — that miserable December
you buried your father.
Blow it out, you'll forget again.

But the dead don't stay dead.

Mother and Father, conspiring behind the door,
dimmed the chandelier in the dining room
where you sat, a child at the head of the table,
in your pinafore, your paper party hat,
feigning surprise as the solemn
procession sang "Happy Birthday,"
your future lighting up before you.

There were fewer candles then.
You could blow all of them out at once.
But now, dozens of candles —
you can't draw a breath
deep enough to extinguish them all.

Gasping, you stand like a fool
before the growing years of your past
and the dwindling years of your future —
choking on smoke, putting out wildfires
while fresh ones spring up around you.

MY FATHER'S VISITS

After she died, we told him, repeatedly,
to think of our house
as his. By seven, he was fully dressed
in slacks and a laundered shirt.
He made his own breakfast,
carried his coffee cup to the sink, and washed it.
He never opened the refrigerator
without asking our permission first.
All day he sat on the sofa, reading.
He reeled off his lists of medicines, blood counts,
tagging along to the grocery, post office,
the kindergarten at three-fifteen,
grateful for any excuse to leave the house.

Suppose my father comes back again.
Suppose he comes back, not briefly —
as when the dead show up in dreams —
but on an open return ticket.
I'm sure I'll feel shy, tongue-tied, and formal,
the way I did when I ran into my old lover
years after we'd broken up.

I won't ply him with questions
about life on the other side.
I'll put clean sheets on the sofa bed.
All the jokes I've saved up to tell him —
I'll knock myself out to make him laugh.
Every morning I'll squeeze fresh orange juice,
fry two eggs over easy, just the way he likes them,
even when he says to please ignore him,
pretend he isn't here.

UNFORGETTABLE

I'm here to kidnap my beloved aunt
from her apartment in Fort Lee, N.J.,
Flossie, my mother's older sister,
born the year the *Titanic* sank.

But before she'll let me kidnap her,
she hijacks me, steering her spiffy
high-tech walker across the street
into rush-hour traffic to the bank.

Breathless, I plead for her to stop.
Bypassing the flashing ATM,
waving her cane, she makes a scene,
repeating yesterday's, before I came,

when she demanded that the teller
withdraw $5,000 in fives and tens,
and make it snappy, from her account.
The bank called the cops, the cops

called her doctor, her doctor
called me to please come ASAP,
extract her from her apartment house
and move her into assisted living.

She calls her walker her "wagon."
She calls me by my mother's name.
Now that both my parents are gone,
I am the responsible party.

I'm responsible and it's no party.
After accusing her optometrist
of losing her bifocals, my aunt
pocketed his ballpoint pen,

the same pen she uses to sign for
the five grand in soft bundled bills
we stuff into tote bags like robbers.
She's the brains. I'm her accomplice.

They can't arrest us. There's no law
against withdrawing money that is
rightfully yours. Back from the bank,
she's too busy dumping her loot

into a drawer to catch me slipping
her car keys into my purse.
She insists on cooking us dinner.
My mouth waters for her brisket,

the only dish she's famous for.
Instead, she fills a pot with milk,
stirs in a spoon of instant oatmeal,
turns on the gas, opens the fridge,

stares inside, as if she's opened a book
and lost her place. Is she hungry?
Where's her appetite? Come to think of it,
where's her full-length sable coat?

Not in the closet where I saw it last.
Did she throw it down the incinerator
chute along with the garbage bags
she ghost-walks past the corridor's

numbered doors twenty times a day?
Is that fur warming a neighbor's back?
Lost, her husband's star-sapphire ring,
her strand of graduated cultured pearls,

her Chanel handbag, not a knockoff.
Lost, her lovely, sophisticated things.
Where did they go? Misplaced? Stolen?
She won't let strangers inside her door,

no social worker, not even the super.
She points to snapshots of my daughter
among the rogue's gallery on her desk:
"She's very pretty, what's her name?"

She says it again two minutes later.
And says it again five times more.
Though I'm afraid to leave her alone,
I lock the bathroom door against her.

I don't want Auntie to see me cry.
I sit down on the closed toilet lid,
turn on the faucet, flush the toilet,
in case she's listening at the door.

But she isn't. She's where I left her,
humming happily, perfectly in tune,
"Unforgettable."
Unforgettable, that's what you are.

III

DREAM CITY

*One night, Chen Chu dreamt that he was a butterfly. In his dream,
he had never been anything but a butterfly. When he woke up he
didn't know if he was Chen Chu dreaming that he was a butterfly
or a butterfly dreaming that he was Chen Chu.* — Zen koan

I was sleeping in a round room made of stone.
A voice called out, "This is your room. This is your bed."
For months thereafter, I crossed a river
on thoroughfares to a city that seemed familiar.
Most nights I'd return there.
Its turn-of-the-century architecture,
wrought-iron and stone apartment houses,
looked like the buildings on Park Avenue, and Fifth.
Sometimes I dreamed hybrids of buildings
over and over: a library–hotel, a train station–school;
and a department store with a rickety elevator that took me
to the fourth floor, where the dresses were.

In one dream, I caught myself telling someone,
"These are the clothes I wear in my dreams,"
as I opened a closet. Inside were
shoes, jumpers, coats, a green hat with a feather —
my taste, my size, they even *smelled* like me.

And, once, I brought someone along with me from *here.*
Here, where I am when I'm wide awake.
I said, "This is the place I always dream about."

As I fall asleep, my dream picks up in the place
where it left off the night before —
the street, the house, the room.
The next day, I might catch a glimpse of it
superimposed on what I'm *really* seeing —
a shard of light bleeding onto a negative.

In time, I began to see my city,
the basso continuo playing behind the melody
of my everyday life, as a kind of everyday life, too:
its industry, the bustle of its people,
its traffic, its history, its parallel *ongoingness* —

But not long ago, I was traveling
along the Jersey side of the Hudson
where I grew up. I hadn't been back in years:
the woods were gone —
the collapsing docks and broken pilings
had been replaced with high-rent condos, supermarkets, malls,
anthills in the shadow of the Palisades.

The bridge and tunnel traffic was awful.
Instead of taking a bus, I crossed
to Manhattan by commuter ferry.
In the middle of the river, I looked up
at the skyline, the buildings
bronzed by late afternoon light —
like my dream city's light —
the city I'd dreamed since I was twelve —

but I wasn't dreaming.
My husband and daughter were sitting on the bench
on either side of me.
Rows of strangers, too.
Some gazed at the skyline, as I did.
Others read their newspapers, or dozed.

FAMILY PORTRAIT, MINSK, c. 1900

Dead long before my time,
how young they are, how old —
my mother's mother
and my great-uncles and great-aunts —
handsome, well dressed, none over thirty —
posed against a painted backdrop of ruins.

Are they orphans?
Where are the elders, parents —
the snow-bearded patriarch,
that pinched little bird perched on the upholstered
seat of honor beside his zaftig wife?
Where is that generation
that appears in every *other* family's
family portrait, except mine?

At fifteen my grandmother leans away
from the others, toward the frame.
Of the eight, only she
has a name, the name passed down
to me. Jenny. Only she
stares at the lens, straight into my eyes.

That's my teenage daughter's face!
Her same self-possessed expression.
Except for the mutton sleeves
and cinched waist
and heavy hair braided and pinned
like a loaf of challah to her head,
they're so alike they could be twins!
Amazing how the genes for that face,
stored inside those nesting Russian dolls,
skipped two generations.

Don't their boots hurt?
Aren't their backs stiff
from holding still so long?

BODY AND SOUL

> The soul remains attached to the physical body after death for the
> first seven days, when it flits from its home to the cemetery and
> back. This explains why the initial mourning period is one week.
> For twelve months after death the soul ascends and descends,
> until the body disintegrates and the soul is freed.
>
> — *Dictionary of Jewish Lore and Legend*

Which must be the reason why,
lying awake in my mother's bed
the night after her funeral, I caught her
rummaging in the underwear drawer.

What a relief to know
the dead are *expected* to come back —
so seeing them up and about so soon
is no big deal.

If you die, say, in July,
I'd like to think that in the next few weeks,
your soul clings like the bar code
to the book of your body.
Little by little, the label
starts to peel, curling and lifting
until the sticky underside loses its grip.

By Labor Day, your body
can walk your soul on a leash,
yanking it back when it lifts a hind leg
over the perfect green of a neighbor's lawn.

Around Halloween, the soul begins to rise.

Thanksgiving,
it's a kind of beach ball clearing the net.
On New Year's Day, it flips on the trampoline

of the body, bouncing higher and higher
until it shoots through the roof.

As Pesach approaches,
your soul — tied by the ankles —
bungee-jumps from the body,
which, meanwhile, has been attending to
its own messy business in the ground.

How else to explain why
Judah ha-Nasi would suddenly appear
to his family on Friday nights,
dressed in his Shabbat finery,
recite Kiddush over the wine, and vanish?

Or why my mother, just last week,
stood behind me by the stove,
telling me my kugel needs more salt.

Some retired dentist from Great Neck
swears he's photographed a soul leaving its body.
And a deposed countess from Romania
topped *that,*
claiming she's measured its weight in ounces.

On my mother's Yahrzeit,
when our family gathers at the cemetery
to unveil her headstone,
and we're crying, why be sad?
Think of it as a bon voyage party —
a soul at last at liberty
to make its own plans.

GOD'S BREATH

If God can be said to breathe the soul
into each living thing, as he did into Adam,
then the magician we hired
for our daughter's birthday party was like God.

Before performing the rabbit-in-the-hat trick,
before pulling shiny nickels
from Emma's ears,
he got a long skinny green balloon
and pulled it like saltwater taffy,
then put his lips to its lip and blew.

And it grew and grew,
luminous and green, it grew
in its nakedness, and when it was a yard long
the magician knotted it,
and with a few deft flicks twisted it
into a dachshund — buoyant, electric, tied to a leash
of fuchsia ribbon — that bounced
along the floor, bumping after our daughter
on their walks around the house.

Weeks later, cleaning under her bed,
I coaxed it out with a broom —
a collapsed lung furred with dust.
As long as it still had some life in it,
I couldn't throw it away.

So I popped it with a pin.
And God's breath, a little puff
from elsewhere, brushed my cheek.

ON THE WAY BACK FROM GOODWILL

After Uncle Al's final coronary,
Aunt Flossie gave my dad
Al's unworn, tasseled, white
patent-leather penny loafers,

the Florsheim labels still stuck
like chewing gum to the heels.
Shoes my elegant father
was too polite to refuse.

So his brother-in-law's shoes
cured in a closet for twenty years,
soles stiff as planks, until
I boxed them up

with my father's things
and shipped them home,
where side by side
in the dark crawl space

under my roof they idled
for another twenty, enduring
long ice-hatcheting winters
Uncle Al would have hated.

Now the last of him
is gone, with his temper
tantrums, and his bad taste,
and his black eye-patch

that covered the empty
socket of his right eye,
lost in a car crash. And
the thick wad of fifties

he carried in his pocket
to intimidate and impress.
No cheapskate, now I slip
a dime into the stubborn

slot on his loafers meant
for pennies, the way
you'd close a dead man's
staring eyes with a coin

so he won't take you
along with him.
Haven't I already
done my time?

THE CLOTHES SWAP

Erika gets Rhea's red wool coat.
Rhea gets Maya's jacket.
Maya gets my pedal pushers.
On her they look good.
"Goodbye, goodbye, goodbye,"
wave the long silky sleeves
of my aunt Lil's blouse
draped over Helen Rabin's arm.
"Adieu, adieu," I blow a kiss
to Aunt Roz's little black dress.
"Wear it well," I say to Gabrielle.
"See you later, alligator," I tell
Flossie's golf shirts as Charlotte
adds them to her stash.

Once, having this much stuff
meant you were rich,
rich as the Tsar. My family
worked hard to have more
than enough to give away.
Owning a dozen pairs of shoes?
What would their zayde say?
"You only have *two* feet!
A person can only wear
one pair of shoes at a time!"

I watch them walk away,
watch their exodus
from my childhood, the threads
that tie me to my tribe,
their treasure, my trash —
the woven archive of their lives.
Take this gorgeous gray chemise, Susan.
You should live so long.

FUGUE

It was not our story. It was hers.
That's how friends told us to think of it.
It was not our story, it was hers.
In what book does it say that you're
supposed to live until you're eighty?
Our house was hers for the summer.
Our forks and spoons and knives.
She seemed happy waving goodbye.
We said, *So long, take care, enjoy.*
It was not our problem, it was hers.
Her clothes hung in our closets.
Her little boy slept in our daughter's bed,
played with our daughter's old toys.
It was not our sadness. It was hers.
Her sadness had nothing to do with us.
She borrowed books from the library.
Scrubbed the bathtub. Baked a pie.
We were just going about our business.
We were hundreds of miles away.
It was not our madness, it was hers.
She finished the book. Sealed
the letter in the envelope, telling why.
We replaced the bloody floorboards
where their two dead bodies lay.
We stained the new boards to match
the old ones — a deep reddish stain
our daughter first thought was blood
until we told her it was not blood.
And not our desperation, it was hers.
It was scraped, sanded, varnished.
No one can tell. It could have happened
to anyone, but it happened to us.

We barely knew her. We weren't there.
We didn't want to make their tragedy
our tragedy. It was not our story.
They had their story. We have ours.

SCRABBLE IN HEAVEN

They're playing Scrabble in heaven
to pass the time, sitting at their usual
places around the table —
or whatever passes for a table there —
my father opposite my mother,
Uncle Al across from Floss,
husband opposite wife — all four of them
bickering as they did in life —
the Scrabble board laid flat
on the wooden lazy Susan,
as Sunday afternoons they'd play
while dinner was cooking,
or if my mother was too tired to cook,
they'd order takeout from the Hong Kong.

After dinner, they'd resume the game,
a conversation interrupted midsentence;
cigarette smoke rising from ashtrays,
dirty dishes stacked up in the sink,
chopsticks poking from the trash pail.
They never invited me
to join them. So I'd sprawl on the rug,
feeling sorry for myself, and finish my homework;
one ear tuned to Ed Sullivan on TV,
one ear tuned to their squabbling,
which continued even when they consulted
the *Webster's* to check a word,
tucking its red ribbon bookmark between
tarnished gilt-edged pages.

Sunday after Sunday,
the lazy Susan rotating on the table,
the pastel squares checkering the grid,
the light blue squares, the navy, the red,

and the black star on the pink square
in the dead center of the empty board,
and the silky feel of the tiles brushing
fingertips as they selected their letters —
just as I'm doing now, touching these keys —
as their memories of the earth
and all the words they had for them —
daughter niece husband wife sister
tree rock dog salt —
diminish one by one.

SEPTEMBER 9, 1995

Walking the half mile to Charlotte's farm,
the Frost tape rasping "Provide, Provide"
into my earphones, I'll take the shortcut
and drop by Roy and Gabrielle's new house.
This cassette will last an hour at most,
from Peck Hill Road to the Pekin Brook,
and as my soles negotiate the dirt road
a snake crosses my path; I let it pass.
Just yesterday in the woods my husband
found a snakeskin like a beige mesh glove.
And now a Monarch lifts from a milkweed pod
and flits beside me for some twenty yards.
In a week or two, they'll all migrate,
by the thousands, thousands of miles south.
The cassette stops. I flip it to Side B.
I have a friend who's phobic about snakes.
She makes her husband scan magazines
before she reads them, to check to see
if any snakes are lurking on a page.
On walks, he has to scout ahead and say
"fire," their signal if a snake's close, or else
she'll have a panic attack and pass out.
Life's full of little ambushes.
Maples turning red, leaves like brushfires
spilling along the branches. Suddenly
I remember — how could I forget? —
September 9 was my father's birthday.
He would have been eighty today.
It's funny how we remember to forget.
But here's the county's oldest house —
never painted — a burnished driftwood box.
I follow the Pekin Brook until Jack Hill;
the farmhouse sits comfortably in between,

wearing a fresh coat of milky clapboards
and black shutters. I unplug my ears.
Two parked cars. I don't bother to knock.
I've got no housewarming gift, no bread
or salt. It's quiet enough to hear them
breathe: Roy dozing in his easy chair,
Gabrielle in her studio, painting on silk.

GELATO

When Caravaggio's Saint Thomas pokes his index finger
past the first knuckle, into the living flesh of the conscious
perfectly upright Jesus Christ, His bloodless wound
like a mouth that has opened slightly to receive it, the vaginal folds
of parting flesh close over the man's finger as if to suck,

that moment after Christ, flickering compassion,
helps Thomas touch the wound, calmly guiding
the right hand of His apostle with His own immortal left,
into the warm cavity, body that died and returned to the world,
bloodless and clean, inured to the operation at hand
and not in any apparent pain —

to accidentally brush against His arm
would have been enough, but to enter the miraculous flesh,
casually, as if fishing around in one's pocket for a coin —

because it's in our natures to doubt,
I'd doubt what I was seeing, too.

Drawing closer, Thomas widens his eyes
as if to better absorb the injury, his three companions also
strain forward, I do, too,
and so would you, all our gazes straining toward
the exquisite right nipple so beautifully painted I ache to touch
or to kiss it, press my lips to the hairless chest of a god.
His long hippie auburn hair falls in loose
girlish corkscrew curls, the hairs of His sparse mustache
straggle over His upper lip, face so close that Thomas must surely
feel Christ's breath ruffling his brow.

The lecturer closes his notebook and we exit the auditorium.
Conveyed smoothly on the moving sidewalk, as if on water,
but not water,

whooshed through the long, shimmery tunnel connecting
the east and west wings of the National Gallery,
my friend and I hurtle away from the past, that open wound,
and toward the future —

the dark winter colors saturating my eyes suddenly
blossom into breezy pastels of Italy's gelato,
milk sherbet quick-frozen and swirled
into narrow ribbons of cold rainbow
unbraided into separate chilled stainless steel tubs set
under glass in a cooler case:

                          tiramisù, zabaglione, zuppa inglese,
milky breasts whipped, rippled peach and mango, pistachio,
vanilla flecked with brown dizzying splinters of bean,
coffee, caramel, hazelnut, *stracciatella,*
raspberry, orange, chocolate, chocolate mint; silken peaked
nipple risen from the middle of the just barely opened
undisturbed tub of lemon so pale it's almost white,
scraped with a plastic doll's spoon,
scooped and deposited on the tongue,
then melting its soothing cooling balm.